JUST START

Then improve.

Graeme Smith

PUBLISHED ON AMAZON.com
  by
LABYRINTH BOOKS

DEDICATION:

This book is dedicated to my family.

Hele-ly (Ly).
my wife:

Ingrid.
our daughter:

Marie.
my former wife:

Fiona, Natalie and Michael
our children:

Georgie
Michael's wife:

Pearl, Kiki and Martha.
their children:

They have put up with me for many years and I thank them for that.
I hope this gives an insight into what occupied me much of the time.
All have done worthwhile and interesting things without my help.
I congratulate them for their achievements.

INDEX:

A: Start stops.

As in most tertiary institutions, the quality of lecturer varied.
In the third year one 'lecturer/teacher' was different from the others.
The others had ideas, passed on knowledge, were keen for us to learn.
They generally did the kinds of things you'd expect teachers to do.

There were slight exceptions.
One actually used our work as material for a book.
Another was keen for us to do well.
So he'd take home unfinished student paintings.
Then work on them to ensure a good result.
Fortunately this didn't happen for me.

In the third year of my art school course I had a hopeless 'teacher'.
He was a well-respected artist.
He appeared for his classes and suggested something for us to do.

He had few comments about how we did it or what was done.
Quite often he had been drinking and wasn't really able to offer much.
In addition he often arrived late and sometime left early too.
There were even occasions when he didn't arrive at all.

My fellow students arrived late, went early, or to the local pub.
Or some combination of these, including not even coming.

But I was motivated by an artistic career, so I kept turning up.
Although I had to spend a lot time driving.
I was teaching at Carlingford in north-western Sydney.
In evening peak hour traffic to Darlinghurst in the eastern suburbs.

Then drive home west to Parramatta each evening.
It certainly was tempting not to come too.
But I was still motivated by the artistic career, which beckoned.
So I kept turning up, still keen to learn.

Eventually I was the only student present (it was a small class).
With no lecturer to learn from I wasn't prepared to waste my time.
But I didn't know what to do.

One memorable night, I was the only person there.
I had no lecturer to learn from.
And no fellow students either!

I wasn't prepared to waste my time.
I had spent an hour and a half just getting there!

But I didn't know what to do.
I had a problem didn't I?

The first time this happened I stared at my blank canvas for a while.
Then I looked at my paints and noticed a tube of Indian red.
I hate Indian red, I thought, so let's use up some of that.
If I was going to waste paint it was a colour I didn't like and rarely used.
So I mixed the paint with plenty of turps and looked at the canvas again.

But even then I wasn't sure what to do with it.
So I flicked the paint onto the canvas in random splashes.

Splash marks went everywhere.

I looked at that for a while and eventually decided to join the dots.
I considered the shapes created and thought I should colour some in.

So I painted in some of the shapes with more Indian red.
Some white was added and more shapes painted.
I continued working on the painting, but more quickly.
It developed into quite a reasonable abstract painting.

Eventually I decided I was finished.
I had an abstract painting to be sure.
But it was way better than I had imagined at the beginning.

Also I learned something.
I learned that it doesn't really matter what you do at the start.

The most important thing is to actually do something.
You don't even need ideas!

Once you begin, you can alter or change what you have done.
It's better to do something and be wrong, than do nothing.
Mistakes can be corrected, and you learn what not to do also.
I'd solved my problem too!

In that lesson without a teacher I discovered how to get started.
You have now discovered this too – but with words not colours.

I don't know what happened to it.
I wish I still had it for that was my first real painting.

Next week it was the same situation again.
However, I decided against flicking the paint this time.

I shut my eyes and made random marks on the canvas.
Then continued painting with the shapes that resulted.

This was my second painting and I learned something else.
I learned in those two lessons (with no teacher) how to get started.
I learned that it doesn't really matter what you do at the start.

The most important thing is to actually do something.
Your mind works better when there's something for it to work with.
A blank canvas is really uninspiring and for many people inhibiting.
We know great masterpieces were painted on similar blank canvases.

Often we try to solve all our problems before we start.
That's generally too hard.
It's usually unnecessary too for most can be worked out along the way.

Those two lessons were life-changing events for me.
I continued with my course and learned an even more important lesson.
This isn't just how to get started on a painting;
It's how to get started with anything.

Discovery everywhere.

The attitude from the hopeless teacher I used in all classes.
Now I learnt from each teacher.
But in my own way and I developed my own art as a result.

I grew self-confidence to replace innocence and naiveté I began with.
Instead of being diligent, I was passionate and really enjoyed painting.
I continued this attitude into the fourth and final year of my course.

One classmate, who later became a university lecturer, said.
'Have fun and enjoy yourself, but wait until the end of the year.
You have to do what they want you to do.'

I suppose generally he was right.
At most educational institutions you do what lecturers want or you fail.
I thought about that briefly, but not for long.

By now I didn't really care whether I passed or failed.
I was on my way to being an author.
I knew being an author was based on what you did.
Not if you pass a course or not.
Many authors haven't done any courses.
Ohers have failed but it didn't matter!

I kept going as before in spite of the well-intentioned advice.
I had a busy and productive year.
I even had 2 works hung in the Wynne Prize (major art award).

Eventually the end of the course came, and the exams arrived.
I received distinctions in every subject.
So naturally I was pleased and proud of the achievement.

A little further down the track I realized what actually happened.
Thus I learnt another of life's lessons.

Examining students was done as in every other art institution.
In each subject all students had to submit works for assessment.
With printmaking a portfolio was required.

The works are viewed by specialists in a particular subject area.
Each would independently rank the works with one being the lecturer.
The group would compare results for the final mark.

If markers view works where most are similar and one is not.
The different one will almost always be placed best or worst.
With a certain amount of skill and creativity a best placing is likely.
If students do what they wanted their works tend to be similar.
They will also be somewhat like the lecturers.

But my work was different from my classmates.
That is basically why I received those distinctions.
I had to be judged best or worst, but I couldn't possibly be equivalent.

That's how it is in the art world.
If it was medicine or accountancy.
My attitude would have had a different result!

Art failure is non-remarkable, just good or average, the expected.
It's more remarkable to be different or totally inferior.

It doesn't matter what you do at the start.

Anything will do.
As long as you do something.

Because that's really the first task – to start!
Your mind doesn't need much to feed on.
So the next task is to develop whatever was done.

Only when the first step is finished do something else.
Do not be in a hurry either, wait until you stop working.
Don't try to do too much as well.
All you have to do is start!

But where will you actually begin?
Most people think a published book is the start of an author's career.
Authors even think this.
Was driving a long journey what you did first when you got your licence?

But before we get to that what happens to your past?
You want to move to be a well-known and successful author.
So what will stuff that belongs to your past do now?
Nothing except undermine your new status.
You must distance yourself from all that.

The best way is to do it publicly and dramatically.
Find everything that has nothing to do with your new career – the lot.
You no longer need them as insurance in case something goes wrong.
You have momentum with what you've written and they are not part of it.

Before any publication sort out what's relevant to the new career.
Keep anything that represents your new career.
Those you intend to keep and not sell (perhaps your superannuation).
Stuff you give away (relevant to new books) in promotions.

Your notes now are the equivalent of actual cash.
That's because they may be published as a book or as part of as book.
So look carefully at those old notes.
Are there any as good as the latest?
If you are really sure about that then put them aside.

All the rest get burnt.
This increases dramatically the value of what is kept.
In future retain even less.

But be quite objective and single-minded about this.
Your future depends on not letting a single item escape.
If it's not to your latest standard.

Now let the party begin.
Have a party where you live.
Invite your neighbours as well as the press.
Take that lesser stuff out into your front yard, or street if necessary.
Choose a fine week-end morning when there'll be plenty of people about.

BURN them along with anything else you do not need.
Burn each item one at a time.
That takes longer and is more spectacular.

Dress suitably but not weird as you're a responsible and sensible author.

Hold up each item dramatically for all to see.
Then throw it on the fire.
Pretend you are a priest of some obscure faith.
Each sacrifice is accompanied by a ritual.

If asked for your fire permit.
Reply by saying what you are doing.
You are celebrating your turning point as an author by burning your past.

Tell them about your upcoming publication.
Give them a brochure for your publication.
Set up a table so you can sign the brochures.
Invite those people to your book launch.

If the police come because of the fire.
Tell them what you are doing, and invite them too.
If a police officer wants something free – refuse.

When the fire burns out, sweep up the ashes.
Put them in a container you have brought.
Gather your table and the book brochures and move to your house.
Without a glance backward wave to those still gathered at the scene.
You are now on your way to being a famous author.

Your book will be a success.
Years ago I read in the national papers of a well-known Australian artist.

He did something similar, he certainly burnt his old works.

I was just an art student at that time.
But although I remember the event my recollection of details is sketchy.
Not like they would be now.

The important thing is, I've never forgotten this either.
All an author does has magical properties due to the creative process.
Use this common myth to your advantage to embark on your new career.

Could you make a dramatic statement like this?
Where would that take your new career?

Starting as an author.

Some time ago I read an old car magazine (another interest).
I came across a story that might appeal to you.
It's about Alistair Brookham (p70 - 72, 'Sports Driver', issue 6 1990).

Alistair makes model cars for a living!
In fact he makes model racing and sports cars, not just any car
Before he started he raced cars, and was a mechanical draftsman too.
So he did have a good background.
In addition his father was a model-maker, although not professionally.
He knew what workmanship, enthusiasm and dedication achieved.

He made some decisions before starting a model-making career.
He had to decide which car to build (yes just **ONE**).

He also had to consider where he could find buyers.
How much they would be prepared to pay.
Not how much he wanted – well not then anyway.

Before picking up any tools, Alistair did a huge amount of research.
He studied books and every available drawing and photograph.

Then back in 1982 he started building two models.
He chose Ferrari racing cars for he was sure there'd be some interest.
Following exhaustive research and relying on his drafting background.
Alistair draws every component to the exact size he will make it.

This was not easy as he mainly works from photographs.
They may not show accurate measurements due to distortion.

So sometimes he has to make a part several times to get it right!

Alistair spends about two months on the design aspect.
He draws each part in the order he will assemble them.
He works from seven in the morning until around nine at night.
These days he usually builds five cars a year!
Alistair estimates it takes 800 hours to build a model.

He worked part time on those first two Ferraris, for three months.
However it became obvious that he would have to make it full time.
So his modelling career depended on the success of those first two cars.
They were sold, but there were no repeat sales or even enquiries.
So it was back to the drafting board for Alastair.

In 1986 (4 years later), a sports car magazine ran an article.
On Alistair's cars and the subsequent interest set the ball rolling again.
The demand for his work is now considerable.
He has a large library these days too.

When I read the article he had enough work for the next ten years.
Alistair asks for a considerable deposit and also cash prior to delivery.
His clients range from museums to investors and enthusiasts.
One thing they have in common is an ability to pay a price tag.
It's a price that relates to the time, effort and skill that goes into the car.
Right from the start Alastair was focused on his potential clients.

Alastair does a great deal of research before starting.
Such as black and white studies, colour sketches, and small trial pieces?
There are artists who do this for each work that becomes a print.

Most authors toss off a book and expect people to buy it.
People will pay just because the author has produced the book.
That's even though it was done to meet their personal creative needs.
Such an attitude is amateurish and doesn't deserve any encouragement.

Perhaps there's no need to put in 800 hours on a book?
Or work full time and do only five per year!
But imagine what you'd produce if you did?

Analyze your approach to your writing.
That means you can work out whether you are truly a professional.
You no longer write just for enjoyment **BUT** also to earn money.

Eventually at your first publication you pull out all stops to sell lots.
You only get one chance to do this!
If your preparation is right it can happen.

Then people WILL remember it for a long time.
Underscore their memory at the end of the publication.
Have another burning of old stuff.

Write something specific.

As an author there's a message for you from Alastair Brookham.
The better background you have the greater your chance of success.
But even with this you still need a professional attitude.
But Alastair did a great deal of research.
So how much research do you do?

Just write stuff BUT DO NOT worry about how it turns out.
Your research is just writing stuff often.
For over time it improves.
But maybe you don't believe this?

Here is a true story.
Years ago I tested a program called Coach Creativity Skill.
In an elementary school.

The pupil challenge was to see what they could do.
With any material combination.
Often, but not always, this included paint.

One teacher noticed a particular boy over a series of lessons.
In the earliest lessons there was always 2 blobs present in the work.
It didn't matter what he was given by the teacher.

Over a period of time the blobs gradually changed into two birds.
Just basic symbol-type birds, such as most people might do.
As the lessons continued the birds improved with more details.
Eventually they became recognizable.

The teacher realized the boy created budgerigars each time.
It didn't matter what materials he was given.
That became a challenge for the teacher.
He tried to find a combination of material that couldn't be budgerigars.

The boy always found a way to make the birds.
One time he even pin-pricked budgerigars onto paper.

Do you think he might be the best budgerigar artist in the world?
If he continued, I'd say every chance.
He was also becoming a creative thinker, which the teacher wanted.

Why did he do this?
Well the teacher discovered (surprise) he had two pet budgerigars.
They meant more to this boy than anything else.
Because the teacher **DIDN'T** tell him what to do.
He could express his feelings and knowledge.

That's how it should be learning to write too.
Just do it and your writing will improve if the motivation is strong enough.
It's also how to develop confidence!

I know a lady who as a girl she sketched the people she saw on TV.
She just did this continually.
She can now draw and paint people superbly.
She is an artist in the fashion industry these days too.

B: Mistakes.

What is your attitude to making mistakes?
There are many people who hate making mistakes.

Often people think they can learn from other people's mistakes.
But the lessons are never the same.

We can never have another's experience.
There's a tendency to repeat the same mistake, if the lesson isn't learnt.
Many people's love life is a testimony to the truth of this assertion.

Learn from a mistake and you're unlikely to repeat it.
You are changed too and cannot return to your pre-mistake self.

When you try to learn from others you are not usually changed.
So it is easy to return to a past behaviour.
A mistake made and learned from and you're changed.
You gain wisdom.

By making mistakes we learn.
We learn the consequences of what we do.
If you avoid making mistakes, that's probably the biggest mistake of all!
Do nothing and learn nothing.

Mistakes are ways to learn something you didn't know before.
We don't want to make mistakes.
But are not afraid if that's what happens.

Our own mistakes are special to us.

They are part of our lifelong learning.

We are wiser, more determined and better due to the experience.

Yes you learn by making mistakes.

You shouldn't be afraid to make a mistake, seem foolish, or be wrong.

Just do what seems to make sense and then see what happens.

If necessary you can modify what you've done.

Then see what happens next.

Eventually you have learned something.

Usually it will be considerably better than whatever you started with.

It's a process of continual improvement.

A teacher didn't understand.

I tested an art education program in the 70's.
Various schools had programs like parts of this book.
Teachers used the suggested materials to see if there were problems.
I'd turn up from time to time to find out what had been discovered.

One teacher said his class couldn't use the suggested materials.
He challenged me to show him otherwise.

He had followed the program.
Although he didn't really understand it.
In any school this is always likely so his feedback was valuable.

I looked at the materials he had assembled.
Lumps of concrete, broken school chair legs, and a big ball of string.

Certainly not a promising combination I thought.
I suggested going outside.
That was to avoid damage to furniture from the concrete.

I spaced the children out and issued the material as suggested.
The lumps of concrete were first.
The students looked at them.
They picked them up and turned them around but they didn't do much.
Well what can anyone do with a lump of concrete?

Then I issued a piece of broken chair leg.
These were arranged with or balanced on the concrete.
But still not much – just a little bit more.

A piece of string came next.
Then later another piece of broken chair and after that - more string.
None were put off by the strange materials.

Eventually those kids made an amazing range of things.
Included was a concrete lump seated on a swing.
There was a dead pet rock and in its grave as well.
Most were of a sculptural nature.

Why did this happen?
As mentioned this teacher had been following the program.
Although he didn't really know what he was doing!
He was just giving out stuff.

His students had learnt from their experiences though.
They could think creatively.
That's why they weren't fazed by the concrete and chair legs.
It was just stuff to see what you could do with.

There was an influence of the environment on student outcomes.
What was done outdoors was different to what they might do inside.

But mainly they were not afraid to make mistakes!

Golfers.

Most successful professional golfers say the game is 95% mental.
Lesser golfers find this hard to believe.
They pay professionals to show how to hit the ball, stand properly, etc.

The report was about research done at the University of Chicago.
Professional and amateur golfers were compared.
Brain activation of the two golfing groups showed different areas.
Some highly active in the amateurs but almost silent for professionals.

These areas were related to motor planning and execution.
An area that co-ordinates sensory input with emotions.
A focus on cognition, movement co-ordination and voluntary movement.
Both were highly active in the amateurs but not the professionals.

These were active as amateurs took too long and unable to focus.
They might have been more anxious about the shot than professionals.
Too much data inhibits motor planning and performance.

The amateur is thinking that each shot is a new shot.
Whereas the professional knows they're the same as previous shots.
They have already been internalized.

Their game is mental as a focus on physical aspects is uneeded.
The amateur has to consciously consider each shot.
This is consistent with learned skills (the authors do not make this point).

Professional golfer's skill are such they don't need to focus on that.

Thus there is little or no relevant brain activity.

Their actions have become almost automatic.

They focus on other aspects of the game.

Like pin placement, slope of the green etc.

But the amateur has too much to focus on and think about.

That means they do not have time for the mental aspect of the game.

You'll understand this better if I relate it to driving a car.

When you learn to drive, everything has to be explained.

You think through the process of driving almost in words.

I'd better brake here, turn the indicator, now, and so on.

Eventually your skill levels improve and you are a better driver.

What also happens is you don't need to talk your way through each step.

You just do it.

The better you get, the less you think (well consciously anyway).

AND the faster you can respond to whatever circumstances that arise.

Just imagine you have to actually talk your way through an intersection?

You'd have an accident for sure – just about every time!

Talking is too slow so it's an inefficient method for guiding actions.

But you don't drive without any thought at all.

If you did you'd still have accidents.

People who have become skilled drivers have internalized their thinking.

What happens is their thinking has become non-verbal

This is faster and more efficient than language thinking

In many sports things happen quickly, we can see the evidence.

The top batsman hooks the fast bowler to the fence.

A leading soccer player angles the ball past the keeper into the net.

Neither of these actions is accidental or unintended.

Yet a player couldn't think it through in words in time to perform the act.

When you drive a car it's exactly the same and in golf it's the same too.

In fact learning and applying ANY skill happens this way.

Think about a child learning to walk.

The child just does it, without concern for what might happen.

The child is unaware of the consequences of failure and thus unworried.

The pro golfer is also unworried and thus confident.

What would happen if golfers were first taught the mental aspects?

Such things as pin placement etc.

That's instead of the skills?

Would they learn the skills anyway?

Would they just do it!

Would they become better golfers?

The archer hits the target, partly by pulling and partly by letting go.

I remember reading this many years ago (and I can't remember where).

The professional has learnt the art of letting go.

It comes with experience, skill and confidence.

Rule of life.

The lesson from the hopeless teacher's class, guided my life.
Doing something, even if random, is better than doing nothing.
You can learn and grow.

It doesn't matter what you do, the most important thing is to start.
Once you begin, you can alter or change what you've done.
But at least something happens.

So you can, and usually will, build on it.
I'm actually doing it now with this book.

Often we try to solve all our problems before we start.
That's generally too hard.
Perfectionism is a waste of time too.

Working things out along the way is better.
Then you embark on a process of continued improvement.
This will lead to highs never even imagined by the perfectionists.

This is also the Bill Gates (Microsoft) approach!
There is no need to procrastinate on anything.

Once you act on an idea, it's tested in the real world.
Your idea is held up and inspected.
It will stand or fail, or maybe even both, but in different ways.

You can then take further action.
Modify those things that need modifying.
Develop those other things that can be developed.

An idea is improved and usually greater than the original thought.
Which otherwise would remain as an untested idea.
Where you end up, won't be random either.
It'll be considerably better than you imagined in the beginning.

It's better to do something and be wrong, than do nothing.
Mistakes can be corrected.
You learn what not to do at the same time.
With experience and confidence later starts improve on earlier ones.
But even then you must start.

Once I attended a course.
Initially I studied and was diligent.
But gradually I followed my own path.

A classmate said 'It's all right having fun and enjoying yourself.
But wait until the end of the year.
You have to do what they want you to do!'

I suppose generally he was right.
At most educational institutions you have to do what lecturers want.
Or you fail.
I thought about that briefly, but not for long.

I didn't really care, whether I passed or failed.
I was on my way to being an author.
One thing I knew was being an author was based on what you did.
Not whether you'd passed a course or not.

Many authors haven't even done formal courses.
Others have failed but it didn't matter!
I kept going as before, in spite of the well-intentioned advice.
I had a busy and productive year and my development moved nicely.

The end of the course came, and the exams arrived as well.
When the results came out I received distinctions in every subject.
Naturally I was very pleased and quite proud of the achievement.

Down the track I realized what had actually happened.
This process was used for examining students.
They had to submit two or sometimes three items in each subject.
Sometimes a portfolio was required.

The submissions are then viewed by a panel of examiners.
They are specialists in a particular subject area, one being the lecturer.
Each independently ranked items from best to worst.
The group compares results for the final mark.

They were faced with fairly similar items and a different one.
Because most students have 'done what they wanted you to do'.
Their items will tend to be similar and somewhat like the lecturers.

Thus the different one will be placed as best or worst.
With some skill and creativity a best place is more likely.

This is basically why I received those distinctions.
My items were different from my classmates!
I had to be judged best or worst, but I couldn't possibly be equivalent.

That's how it is in the literary world too.
The art world is the same!
In medicine, or accountancy, I would've had an entirely different result.

So the main point from my experience is this:
In literature it's more important to be different from other authors.
Than it is to be the same.

Now I was confident about myself as an author.
But in the following years my literary endeavours were diverted.
I followed an educational pathway.

You do different things according to motivation and knowledge.
Decisions based on superficial understanding can affect all that follows.
You really do owe it to yourself to weigh everything up all the time.

I'm not complaining for in life there's always choices to be made.
The important thing is to make them and then get on with it.
Generally I have done that.

My interest in psychology, philosophy, sociology, and education.
Meant I actually went to university to study such matters.

I've written books and developed programs in art education too.
These are for both children and adults.
Later when I ran my gallery I used this information to help me there.
With what I was doing and also with my teachers.
That's when I also began reading extensively in the marketing area.
All this came from my consulting with the Education Department.

Teaching is part of the business of art.
Teaching is also a commercial option for an author.
This can be an addition to writing or any other literary activity.

Not all authors want to teach but many do.
You choose whether to become involved or not.
BUT if you do you're probably in business.
Then business principles apply to teaching.

I was a teacher before I became an author.
But you can do it the other way around and I've done that too.

It's hard to paint and teach without compromise John Hill (UK).
John says successful teaching requires creativity and hard work.
Often this is to the detriment of the teacher's own art.
Students influence a teacher technique, style, palette, or subject matter.

But some well-established authors teach.
Their teaching is usually based on their personal writing skills.

Whether to specialize or not, is a choice authors have.
Anyone can specialize.
Maybe in a media, particular subjects, or style.
Teachers can do the same.

But what you can't do is both specialize and not specialize.
The beginner author tends to try all ideas, media, topics and so forth.
A beginning teacher often does this too!
They have to do this to find out what they like and do best.

Some authors even do this for a very long period.
They become life-long students.
Nothing wrong with that either!

But many discover certain things interest them more than others.
They tend to follow this interest.
Nothing wrong with that either.
Teachers can do the same.

Because of their focus, they get better at their specialty.
They apply knowledge and experience with depth and understanding.

Delegation is the key to leveraging yourself.
You get other people to do things for you.
So an author can have an agent.

Business has an awareness of the importance of delegation.
Used effectively it's possible to increase income and free time.
Do what you do best and delegate or discontinue anything else.
Time on tasks of lesser value is inefficient use of time and energy.
Delegate any tasks that can be performed by a person earning less.
That frees time to focus energy on tasks worth $50 per hour or more.

Delegate to people who have competence in a specific field.
People who know more.
Are more efficient and carry out tasks in less time.
In my case it's worth paying an accountant.

But define the task clearly.

What is your intended outcome?

Be clear about what you want the person to do.

You'd like an agent, but what exactly do you expect them to do?

Then start looking for someone who can and is willing to do that.

Find the person for the task.

Ask THEM to repeat the details of the task IN WRITING.

Is their description an accurate description of what you want done?

If not explain the differences in detail.

AGAIN submit their understanding IN WRITING.

The writing step helps enormously in achieving buy-in.

It also helps to make sure you get the outcome you want.

Otherwise they do what they think you want.

This may not be the same.

Discuss and get agreement on the resources to achieve the task.

There's a major problem if you've hired an agent.

AND they submit invoices for travel and accommodation.

But keep your word regarding consequences.

These steps could be used by someone who wants to commission a work. Convert the steps into a written guarantee.

C: Discovering creativity.

I demonstrated teaching methods I had developed.
I'd teach a lesson, and point out others in a handout (became a book).
Teacher groups had ifferent lessons, so they could share experiences.

An improvement was start a lesson and suggest its end.
Then continue with one of those alternative endings.
The teachers had experienced two lessons rather than one.
I continued and sometimes three, or more, were in the one session.

Gradually I became aware of something unexpected.
The teachers stopped listening to what I said.
Instead they became involved in what they were doing.
It was a startling and unexpected discovery.

The teachers were exhibiting creativity!
I could recognise the behaviour due to my reading and thinking.
But I was not expecting to find it in those in-service sessions.
They were meant to gain an insight into some lessons!
So I started to think about what had happened.

Why were the teachers behaving in this way?
Obviously I had done something to cause it, but what?
Lessons from my hopeless art teacher was part of the answer.

But I really didn't discover creativity, it was there all the time.
Others have made extensive studies into creativity and creativeness.

At the time of my discovery I had read quite a few of these.
So at least I had some ideas what creativity was.

I'd also done some thinking of my own too.
That indicated to me the importance of creativity in relation to art.

Put simply, without creativity there is no art!
That doesn't mean other things aren't needed too.
BUT there is no such thing as non-creative art.
It simply doesn't exist.

But if creativity was all that art is.
Then there would be no way to distinguish art from music.
Or literature, dance and similar areas.
There are some differences, or they are all the same!

I had discovered creativity when I wasn't expecting to.
That discovery eventually led me to how to coach creativity skill.

Here is what happened (next page):

Initial materials

Next material
Does something

Does   something
more
Next material

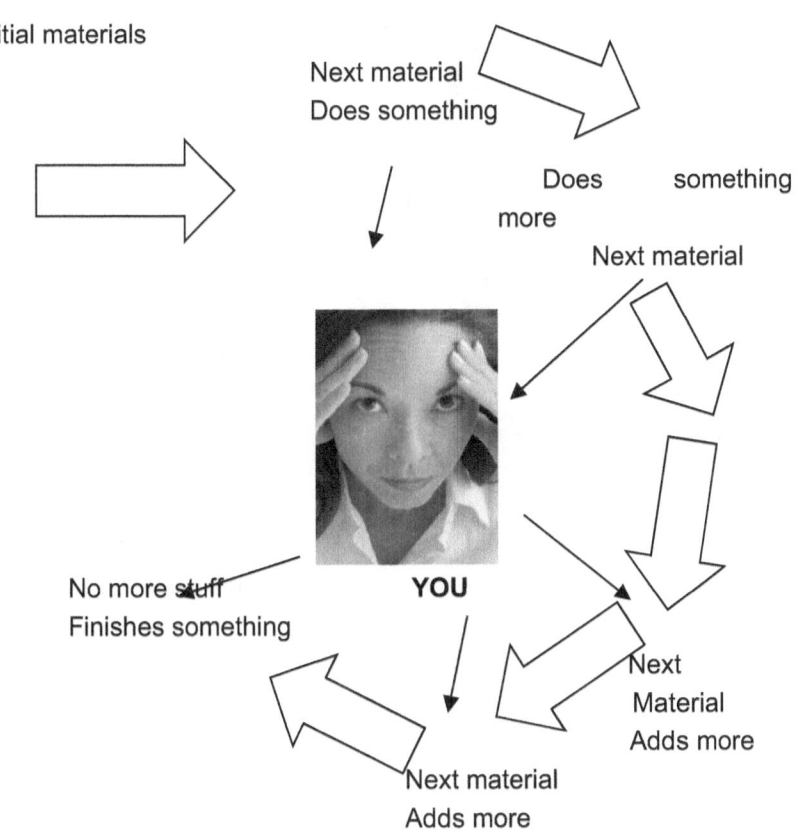

No more stuff
Finishes something

YOU

Next
Material
Adds more

Next material
Adds more

Skill takes time.

For some it takes a lot of time to develop.
When children learn a sport, or read, or paint it is obvious.
Adults learning the same things tend to be impatient.
They tend not to allow sufficient time for skill to develop.

The sport of body building illustrates what could take place.
An athlete completes many lifts of weights over a lengthy time period.
Small increments of additional weight are applied at regular intervals.
Eventually a weight-lifter has the strength to lift very heavy weights.
Impossible weights at the beginning of the training process.

Skill is practiced behaviour.
That's what an experienced weight-lifter has done.

What if you wish to develop a higher level of skill?
The best way is many repetitions allied to small increases in difficulty.
Just like the weight-lifter!

A California author wanted to learn how to paint polar bears.
His painting skills were quite modest too.
I suggested he do many small studies by looking at photographs.
It didn't matter if he finished or not.
They were ways to learn about bears.

After 250 studies he did his first painting with no polar bear.
Not even a photograph.
He was totally surprised at how well his polar bear turned out.

The standard of the work was way better than in the past too.
He had internalized his learning.
The polar bear he created was his not a photographer's.
They were his!

D: Do you write?

Maybe just some words on a mobile phone.
Or a text message.
Probably you've never thought about writing a book either.

BUT here's what you could do.
Just record some thoughts, maybe on your phone.
Do **NOT** worry about how they are written.

Get them down before they disappear.
If necessary get someone to translate this into a written format.
Then add more thoughts.
Keep going like this and

Eventually you'll have enough thoughts for a book.
A book that will sound like you too.
Because it has the same words you use.
The same way.

So writing a book is actually the easy part.
Just do it in a series of small steps.
The main thing is for your style to be consistent.
If it's always you talking then your style IS consistent.

Publishing your story is different.
But promoting your book is actually the most difficult aspect of all.
The next chapter helps you with that.

Amazon.com offers some error correcting.

But it accepts the style you use.

Amazon.com accepts whatever you actually write too.

So **YOU** are responsible for what is written.

Start your book:

You can start a book on Amazon THEN change what you have written.
Amazon accepts whatever you write at any time.
But it **ONLY** publishes the latest version.

So you are responsible for what is written.
This is a major difference from other book publishers.
There your book **MUST** be right **BEFORE** it is published!

Install and open an Amazon.com account to start publishing.
Go to Amazon Kindle Direct Publishing.
Follow the prompts to register.

Once you are registered select "Choose File".
This opens your book file.

Now open your bookshelf.
Click on Create a New Title (upper left)

Commence with a paperback book.
After that you can download to a Kindle ebook easily.

Spend time getting the Amazon details page right.
Eventually the Amazon details page is correct.

Once you complete your eBook details page.
Go to the next page.

Scroll down and then click:
"Upload paperback manuscript" to upload your content.
Browse to the file of your book content and click to upload.
If you've uploaded click "Approve."

Go to "Cover Creator" to create or change the cover.
Click "Save and Continue".
To go to the "Paperback Rights & Pricing" page.
If you've uploaded a paperback update click "Approve."
Click "Publish" at the bottom of the page.

Interior: Book details:
Make sure the information in your interior and cover files exactly match.
The book details (e.g., title, author name, ISBN, language)

Compare the book details you entered during title setup.
With the information in your manuscript and on your cover.
Be sure to check all locations where book details appear.
For example copyright page, headers, etc.
The information in your interior and cover files MUST exactly match.

If the details in your manuscript file don't match.
Correct any differences, including minor ones.
Like author name John T. Smith in book details.
AND J.T. Smith on title page.

Check all locations where book details appear.
Such as the copyright page and headers.
Update your book details or upload your revised file to KDP.

To edit a previously published book.

Click the ellipsis button ("...") next to the book you want to edit.
Select "Edit Paperback Content."

Amazon.com is different.

Initially Amazon only published ebooks.
They are electronic books with **NO** actual printed material.

The Amzon.com eBook system was later adapted for books.
A later innovation is different paths for novels and text/reference books.
My books were published before that.

A publisher publishes AND sells books.
Publishers earn money by selling books.
A printed a book can't be changed.
So editing is done **BEFORE** publication.

Amazon.com does publish physical books too.
BUT they are printed versions of eBooks.

So Amazon.com book publishing is different.
It's based on the eBook system Amazon.com uses.

Which means ALL are ELECTRONIC.
Thus Amazon.com sells titles **NOT** books.
Amazon.com has a huge store of electronic books.

There are advantages for authors as a result.
That's if you know of and use the opportunities provided.
This book helps you do this.

Rights.
You keep control of your rights and set your own list prices.
You can make changes to your books at any time.

WHERE NEXT:

You might consider publishing your story.
Then go to this link:
http://www.amazon.com/dp/B087DWKPTP

NOT NOW:

Perhaps this book could interest you then?

Find out by downloading this book:

http://www.amazon.com/dp/B086Y6K1HZ

SEND TO:

Know anyone interested in chocolate recipes?
They can get this book:

http://www.amazon.com/dp/B0882HK9Q9

APPENDIX:

CAREER SUMMARY:

Summary of creative enterprises commenced:

Founder Riverina Galleries, Wagga Wagga 1979 - 1997.

Founder of Riverina Framing (from 1980-90).

Developed ArtPak a correspondence course for authors (1995)

Published 'Art Professional' newsletters for authors.

Author "SPACE Art Education" for primary schools NSW (1970 - 1982).

Summary of creative enterprises commenced with others:

Art consultant with NSW Department of Ed. from 1970-77 (Sydney).

Founder NSW Art Education Association (1970)

Art consultant with NSW Department of Ed. from 1980-81 (Riverina).

Consultant curator Charles Sturt University (1985-94).

Partner in Business Thinking Systems, Wagga Wagga (1999-2004).

Summary of related activity:

Graduate Bathurst Teachers College (1955).

Graduate National Art School (1970) distinctions ALL final year subjects

Graduate Macquarie University (1979)

Taught general studies, art, art education, art philosophy.

In pre-school, infants, primary, secondary, university, adult education.

2 works hung Wynne Prize (1969) (major Australian landscape award).

Won various art awards and had 22 one-man publications.

Judged art shows in various parts of Australia.

Writes in 'Australian Author' magazine each month, since 1995.

Writes in 'International Author' magazine each two months, since 2002.

Wrote 'Coaching Creative Hockey' published NSW Sport & Rec. (1974)

Coached Parkes Magpies, Parkes, Sydney University, NSW University.

Selector Parkes, Sydney, NSW hockey.

Deputy President NSWHA.

Founder MG Car Club of Wagga Wagga.

Founder Gathering of the Faithful MG Car Club of Wagga Wagga.

www.ingramcontent.com/pod-product-compliance
Lightning Source LLC
Chambersburg PA
CBHW030531220526
45463CB00007B/2779